Poems and more Poems by Ren

Poems and More Poems

by Ren

Matador
9 Priory Business Park,
Wistow Road, Kibworth Beauchamp,
Leicestershire. LE8 0RX
Tel: 0116 279 2299
Email: books@troubador.co.uk
Web: www.troubador.co.uk/matador
Twitter: @matadorbooks

ISBN 978 1785892 684

British Library Cataloguing in Publication Data.
A catalogue record for this book is available from the British Library.

Printed and bound in the UK by TJ International, Padstow, Cornwall
Typeset in 11pt Baskerville by Troubador Publishing Ltd, Leicester, UK

Matador is an imprint of Troubador Publishing Ltd

With love and gratitude to Bar, my SMLCF
and our extraordinary family.

I have received a great deal of encouragement and support from my friends; far too many of you to name but I hope you know who you are. I am truly grateful to you.

However particular thanks must go to Chris Doncaster who managed to persuade me that a wider readership might actually like my poetry.

Heartfelt thanks also to Margaret Hyde, without whose patience and downright hard slog my manuscript would never have got to the publishers and to Bridget and Adrian Plass, who enjoy my poetry and are willing to say so.

Contents

Introduction

I am often asked if my poetry reflects my life. When this happens I can be fairly sure that, having read the brutal realism portrayed in some of my poems, the reader has jumped to the conclusion that they all speak of my own experience. If this were true I really would be a sad and cynical old lady, which I'm not. No, honestly, I'm not!

What those particularly difficult poems offer is a small insight into every human life. Does anyone escape periods of illness, injury, loss, disappointment and despair? But then there is the other side of life; the joy, the fun, the hope and I believe, the healing and redemption.

I hope that you will find something in this little book with which you can make a connection. Something that will speak to you and give you hope. Or a laugh.

Ren
January 2016

The Granny Gap Year

In 2005 both my Beloved and I had to retire from work due to ill health. We would take a Granny Gap Year, enjoy nature and be creative!

We rented an old converted boat on South Beach, Heacham, just a wooden shed really and moved in with our dog and cat.

Over the following year we came to know some of the real beauty of Norfolk. I grew sicker as my failing kidneys gave up the fight and at the end of the year it was no longer feasible for us to move back to Yorkshire. I started dialysis, went on the transplant list and we moved to nearby Hunstanton.

However it was no hardship to stay and this first selection of poems reflects my growing delight with our new home.

A Norfolk New Year

When pinkfoot geese adorn the winter sky
And graceful barn owls sequence dance the field.
When snowdrops clothed in deepest slumber lie
Until to springtime's womb the winter yields.
Here on the cusp of this year and the next
The future closely draws its curtains round,
Forbidding me a view of things to come.
I listen for the future. Hear no sound.
For many years I have replayed this scene
As, trembling on the verge of what shall be,
I stand. At loss and sorrow such a sad old hand.
And yet again and yet again,
The seasons paint the backdrop of my life.
And so the beauty of a winter's day,
Or the restless fecund glory that is Spring,
Stirs up my flesh and so once more
I fling the old year's door far open wide
And bid the New Year in.

Heacham

Living on South Beach 2005-2006.

I've travelled far in miles across the years.
Seen many a glorious beach and thundering sea.
Yet wake each morning oh so glad to find
That Heacham's healing peace now nurtures me.

There is a magic here, so I have found.
An alchemy of sky and sand and sea
That casts a spell upon my heart and mind
That Heacham, Heacham is the place to be.

Is it in the cry of migrant bird
Or whispered by the east wind in my ear?
Or is the message carried by the waves?
I only know the truth of what I hear.

For I have found the peace that I have sought
In tides and skies unfurled for me to see
The Artist's brushwork on the canvas of my life
And Heacham, Heacham is the place for me.

Hunstanton Prom

The winter tide turns landward, covering sand
Left cold and careless by the east wind's hand.
And runs, an eager lover, up the beach
To kiss Hunstanton Prom's wide, arm stretched reach.

The winter visitor blinks her watering eyes
And peers with admiration at the skies
That cloak, with daily beauty, this quiet place
And whispers 'stay' to every upturned face.

Stay. Embrace a sight which, heaven sent,
Grants every willing soul a deep content.
A peace that youthful bustle can't provide
A peace that soothes the soul on every tide.

Brancaster Staithe

What do they sing to each other
Those dinghies on Brancaster Staithe
As if urged by the sweep of the tiller
And scored by the wind and the waves?
There's the high clinky clink of the trebles
And the low clunky clunk of the bass,
Do they sing of last weekend's endeavours,
Or look forward to next weekend's race?

Do they sing a capella in winter,
Sweet carol the incoming geese,
Rehearsing for Spring's intervention
Their full choral work to release?

When the halyards will leap to attention
As each mast feels the beat and the pound
Of the sails, as in pure exaltation
They give voice to a wonderful sound.
The anthem they sing to each other
Those dinghies at Brancaster Staithe,
The chorus so joyful and flighty
To a score by the wind and the waves.

Blickling Hall

There is no silence even here
Where sun blessed acres, far from town,
Create a picture so divine
That every sense serves to combine
A memory that may still be saved
Far into the future, for some darker day.

On the breeze are carried sounds of birdsong
Sweet and clear. And happy children's voices
Which, when I hear them takes me
Way, way back to so much earlier days
On my life's track.

I hear again my children's uninhibited cries
And see their lovely faces in my memory's eye.
Their sturdy little limbs, their tousled hair
And somehow live again the joy of being there
On sun-kissed days. That perfect God blessed bliss
Which I have briefly lived again
Because of this.

The Balance of Nature

We gaze at them and wonder at their movement,
Their voice, their habitat, their hue.
And they look back at us, anxious in their looking.
Survival is their aim,
Do we not also play that game?
And when they look at us might it not be
That what they see is nature too?

And if strangers to our planet came
Intent on taking stock of all that lives.
Lets say 'all nature' for the sake of this,
And studied with non-prejudicial eye
Weighing all who walk the earth
Gainst those who roam the sky.
Might they not judge that all they see
To equal be?

Man Shed

This little poem is written for all the man-shed men we have had the joy of knowing; Peter, David, Lou and many others.

At the bottom of the garden
Tucked in behind the bins
There's a little wooden palace
Where I keeps me little sins.
There's a pack o' special bakky,
Some cans o' favourite beer,
A place where I can sit and dream,
Where worries disappear.
A place where I can cogitate
Those things wot I ave done.
Those things I'd clout me sen for doing
If I ad been me son.
But then, I'm not so I can see
My man shed is the place for me.

The Gardener's Revenge

Rumble, rubble, soil and grubble
In the garden there is trouble.
Down among the growing taters
Lurk the gastropodic gators.
Jaws wide open, munching, crunching.
On the strawberries now lunching.
BUT!
Down the central reservation
Past the compost conurbation
Feathers rattling, all a-preen
Comes that Fowl. The Quacking Queen.
And with glee she slams the brakes on
As her greedy eye delights on,
What is this she's found to munch on,
Ducks love big fat slugs for luncheon!

Jacob and Reuben go Karting at Swaffham

Jacob and Reuben are out on the kart track
Racing their Mother from corner to straight.
Splashing through puddles, avoiding close huddles
Where crunching and crashing might force them to brake.

Down comes the rain like a tropical storm,
Blinding their eyesight and soaking their skin.
There's pain in their hands, their feet and their backsides.
To two watching grannies it seems rather grim.

But look at their faces, so flushed with excitement,
The joy of the speed and the love of the chase,
As over and over, despite the conditions
Each puts down his foot for the thrill of the race.

Marj's Party

In summer, year on year we meet,
The friends of Marj each other greet
And gather up the strands of time
In conversation, food and wine.

What have you done? Where have you been?
Is that your grandchild I have seen?
With words like these, however few,
We bond again our social glue.

And through the journey of that day
Our music to each other play.
Songs from decades past are sung
And memory stirred with sweet, warm fun.

Remember this as winter rears
Its frigid head in passing years.
Next summer waits to bring along
Marj's party. Friendship's song.

Bin Bag Dancing

I saw a cast aside bin bag dancing in the wind
Rejoicing in its freedom, so it seemed.
As leaping, looping, high above, it tangoed through the air.
It looked quite beautiful to me
With my earth-anchored stare.

Across the flattened fen it raced
First fat, then thin and torn.
As though some mighty, unseen hand had chosen to display
Its unimaginable grace to me
Who stood and watched that day.

For quite some time I stood and stared, entranced by what I saw
And for a moment could believe that magic held it there.
But then, with a regretful sigh, the wind released its hand
And dropping, dropping through the air
It fell upon the land.

Across the furrows' clarted mud I trod with heavy tread
And stooping, lifted in my hand the lifeless plastic waste
And with a queasy, shuddering haste, stuffed it in my bag.
And yet I felt a lingering joy and whispered to the wind
My thanks that it could learn to dance before it must be binned.

Traumatic Times but Hope Hangs on

From 2006 onwards, life became considerably more challenging. Dialysis saved my life in the first instance and then, wonderfully and in my case totally unanticipated, I received the gift of a kidney donated by the wife and family of a man called John, complying with his previously declared wishes.

John died suddenly, a tragic accident and I was constantly thinking about him and his family as I experienced the life restoring wonder of organ transplantation. Almost immediately I wrote a poem dedicated to him and continued to record and comment on some of the situations I experienced or observed during frequent stays in hospital.

So here are a few of those observations. I have met some wonderful people occupying beds close by and formed remarkably deep, though transient, relationships. Some lived, some died but I was frequently uplifted and hauled to my feet by the courage and resilience of my fellow patients. I remember them with so much gratitude.

Closed Eyes

I close my eyes
And on the dark side see
Shooting stars and fairy rings
A thousand brief, bright, sparkling things
That simply would have passed me by
Had I not put the lid down on my eye.

Moods

Dark today. Silhouettes in shades of grey
Throw shadows on the backdrop of my mind
And somehow cannot find a single lightening ray.
Yes. Definitely. Dark today.

Glum today. Sad, childlike spectres, seeming quite alone
Who find no-one to play with, no kind home.
Or even ears to listen when they say,
Yes. Definitely. Glum today.

But brave today. Determined. Gritted toothed.
Back against the wall.
Somehow I will keep going, damn it all.
And cling with courage gathered on the way.
Yes. Definitely. Brave today.

For My Donor (John)

I grieve for you, for your life here now ended.
For those who love you, miss you, want you back again.
But thrill with gratitude for life extended.
The Gift you gave, their loss my gain.

We never knew each other, yet connected
We are bound to be from this day on.
Like *sotto voce* singing by my soul detected
The echo of your 'then' my 'now' song.

I pray that you, now freed from time and pain
Will come to know, be comforted, at peace.
And those who loved and lost you also find
The Gift you gave grants them, somehow, release.

Patients Together

We share this space in time.
Hold each other's hopes and fears,
Absorb each other's painful tears
And somehow this contrives
To bandage up again
Our wounded lives.

We watch each other's scene unfold.
Witness another's moment on the stage.
Contribute lines of comedy and rage
And in another's script can dare to say
The words which we ourselves
Might own today.

But in this captured moment, though it be
Difficult at times, so dark and sad,
We also often see ourselves as glad
When laughter lights the shadows of our day
And we with truth and gratitude can say
I'm glad that you were here with me today.

Being Patient in Isolation

I'm just the patient, lying here in this room
With its light loveless walls and its aura of gloom.
As hour after hour through the long day and night
I cling onto my 'being' with all of my might.

I am being as patient as a patient can be.
I am being a 'good girl' and trying to see
That by being compliant and not saying 'NO!'
I'll be being the one who will soon get to go!

But just at the moment, although I'll behave,
I am finding it hard to be jolly and brave.
I am feeling so powerless and fragile and sad
And just a bit scared that I might go quite mad.

One night, perhaps tonight, I'll creep out of my room
And, carrying lipstick, go into the gloom
Of deserted corridors, stairwells and halls
And write "God help the patient" all over the walls.

Lying on the Floor

She barely feels it starting
This spring of misery
That wells up somewhere deep inside
And whispers words to her
Of sad and bleak, unholy things
Of loss and pain and lies.
Until what small joy clings to her
Just gives up hope and dies.

It kicks her heart in passing
On its way up through her chest.
Evolves from spring to river
In one sobbing, gasping breath.
No chance to close the floodgates.
No time to slam the door.
The flood is high. She's drowning.
And she's lying on the floor.

But afterwards? Well afterwards
When wails and sobs subside,
As beached, post flood detritus
She simply wants to hide.
But the air is somehow fresher,
The horizon pale but clear,
And the raging flood within her
Has washed away her fear.

She knows it waits to ambush her
Along some future track.
But now, for just this moment,
Her courage scuttles back
And takes up its position
As the bouncer on the door
To the sanity of this woman
Who is lying on the floor.

Cancer

At first it grips an icy hand around his throat
And cuts his mind off from his trembling whole,
Numbing, flattening the life-line of his spiritual soul,
Rising through his being, flooding fear
That he is going to lose the life he holds so dear.

Before long he is swept aboard the carousel of tests and scans,
The recognised procedures of his plight.
And starts to see that even in this fight
He need not be alone.

And so slowly what was alien becomes less so
As he finds others who are also clad
In armour made to fight this common foe.
His life is led more fully day by day
Sustained by loving ones who pledge to pray
That he will know God's presence
Should he go, or stay.

Ursula demented. Ursula renewed

She weeps dry tears, has shed so many
Over all her years, that now, when in her end time
She yearns for comfort, broken and bereft
Now, when she needs it most, there is nothing left.

No hope. No aid. No friend to whom she'd cling
Plan for a future that's no longer there.
For she is in a 'present' now which was her future
And all there is and will be is the past, which she can't bear.

She cries for a dead husband, now long gone.
A death she mourns for every day
As round and round the loop of memory spins
And somehow will not let her access happier things.

And then he comes. Her grandson, young and strong
And holds her gently. Arms so full of love and on her face
Appears a smile, restoring her to what she used to be
So transfigured that an act of God is clear to me.

And then I see it as it truly is. An earnest from the Lord
A glimpse of how the resurrected Ursula will be
When as she sheds this broken life
Her Lord she'll see.

The Last Lap

Somehow, in these later years,
We have arrived at this.
A place where all our hopes and fears combine
To stand, despite our wintertime.
Can we fling wide that opening door,
The last in life's long corridor?
And put our hopes and fears to bed?
I think not! We must make a stand
And shake off death's stark out reached hand.
And every day find times to laugh.
Yet sometimes welcome welling tears.
Face up with courage to our fears,
Still value every passing day,
And trust You hear us when we pray.

Talking Things Through

When I was still working as a trauma counsellor I met some of our society's most hurt individuals. Victims of practically every conceivable cruel thing that life and other people can perpetrate filled my working day. Their courage was amazing.

Here are a very few of the poems that came out of the experience of working with them. Scribbled on bits of paper during the night or over a relaxing drink at the end of the day, I recognise them as an attempt on my part to process the inevitable feelings stirred up in me by their bravely shared stories.

I include them here because these emotions are ubiquitous and there may be a reader who might feel less alone as a result of knowing that.

Anger Management

Here come the clouds,
Sucked up into the porous surface of my happiness.
Darkening to purple the ceiling of my mood
And through the growing gales of anger
I hear myself disintegrate,
Becoming brusque and rude.

What triggers this down spiralled path?
The fall from grace I dread each bright new day.
Sweeping away the firm, determined thought
That when the grim guys come I will not play.
I fear it's something deep, deep down inside
That mouldy remnant of some long ago mad feast
Which, at the time, I gobbled up with no restraint
Unaware that with the meat, I ate the beast.

What my anger needs is management perhaps.
A way to tame the fury I've ingested.
Withdraw the energy I've given to its growth
And find some peace in which to reinvest it.
So back to the beginning I must go.
Fight the tares and brambles of my mind.
Tame the grumpy beasties that are there
And nurture a persona much more kind.

The Actress

I look in the mirror and what do I see?
A thousand reflections and one of them me.
But which one I am I really can't say,
It entirely depends on the game that I play.

I put on my make-up and pick up my mask.
Dust off my script and get on with the task
Of pleasing my audience, not letting them see
My responses depend on the lines they feed me.

Where is the child, once so honestly wild,
Open and trusting, her dreams undefiled?
Is she prisoner for ever inside the sad mind
Of this woman whose destiny she cannot find?

But then in the mirror I find I can see
A lightening countenance. Could it be me?
As the child I've imprisoned and held down so long
Begins to break out. To grow up. To belong.

And I, in my turn, learn to trust what is true,
That I need not pretend I'm exactly like you.
And all those disguises I needed to be
Are completely discarded and I am just me!

Song for the Inner Child

Does anybody want to listen to the little song that's written
By the child who lives inside my head?
Sometimes she is quite intrusive, disruptive and abusive.
If I could, I'd send her off to bed.
She needs to tell the world about the pain she has endured.
She's tired of being trampled underfoot.
She wants to scream and shout a bit and force us all to see
That she's had enough of 'them' and she's had enough of 'you'
But most of all she's had enough of 'me'.

She can't believe that justice gets a look in.
Or that the fates are ever, ever kind.
She feels she has been doomed from the beginning
To struggle in the darkness, her back against the wall,
With the other grim inhabitants of my mind.
She's fretting and she's fighting and she's struggling to be free
Because she's had enough of 'them' and she's had enough of 'you'
But most of all she's had enough of 'me'.

I'm trying to remind her that I'm always on her side
And that I hold the key here in my hand.
But I'm trembling with fearfulness and anger at her childishness
And lots of other feelings that I really do not like or understand.
I need to let her out into the world.
She needs to leave behind the damaged past
It's time for her to be herself at last
Now is her time to live and love
Now is her time to be
Because she's had enough of 'them' and she's had enough of 'you'
But most of all she's happy now with me.

The Danger of Empathy

Oh the danger of empathy, what it can do
If I walk in your shoes and imagine I'm you.
The minute I do so the danger will be
I'll be thinking like you and no longer like me.
Before very long I'll be feeling your pain
And all my resentments will not be the same
As I see things through your eyes it will open the door
To friendship, forgiveness and quite a lot more
Of those dangerous feelings which would undermine
My previous intention to perceive, all the time,
You as the enemy but now I cannot
Because empathy changes things, rather a lot!

There's No Time

A song

I am driving down the road in the vehicle of life
Changing gear to go faster and braking in strife.
What is my destination? I really do not know.
But of one thing I am certain. I must not go too slow.

Chorus

There's no time. There's no time for the life I call mine.
No space for the dreams just for me.
Dreams of warm sandy beaches and searching for seashells.
And paddling there in the sea.

What is the point of rushing if I leave myself behind?
I love you all most dearly and don't mean to be unkind.
But at last it's dawning on me and it simply must be said
If I don't wind down willingly I'll surely wind up dead!

Chorus

But listen to this warning for it isn't only mine.
There are many of life's drivers playing chicken with their time.
So let's do the things that matter and forget the things that don't.
Be sure of what we will do and reject the things we won't!

Chorus

Ideas

Ideas like dust motes float across my mind.
Some fall, with gentle curses, to the ground.
But some will rise, lit up by beams of light,
Creative halos, new thoughts, shining, bright.

Where do they go then, if I do not catch
Their vision in supporting, skillful hands?
Or warm the embryonic seed of bright new thought.
Using the gift of inspiration as I ought?

Just wasted then the chance of some new thing
And trampled in the dust of tired old dreams.
The choice is mine. And likely too it's yours.
So grasp it lest it's finally slammed
In time's cruel doors.

Cupboards

The corridor of life, be it narrow or wide,
Has so many cupboards in which we can hide.
Where we can pretend we are something we're not
And appear to be 'cool' when in fact we are hot
With embarrassment, anger or scarlet-faced shame.
And we cannot find anyone else we can blame.

When this is our problem the best we can do
Is step out of our cupboard, admit that we too
Are often defensive, dismissive, unkind,
And the more we speak truth then the truth we will find
Is that we are all prey to the trouble and strife
That inhabit the cupboards in the corridor of life!

Still Life

The first poem in this section more or less sums it up.

The poems included here are either moments in the lives of others that I have observed, for example 'Going to the Doctors' or actual events which I have experienced myself.

Sometimes questions have occupied my mind, 'Are there Horses in Heaven?' or events from the past with personal resonance, 'Brown Beauty' for example.

We are in a time of remembrance and the WW1 inclusions directly arise from the deaths of my grandfather and two great uncles in that dreadful conflict.

Still Life

A captured moment caught behind closed doors.
A scene from someone's life,
It might be mine, or yours.
Does it have significance? Who can say.
It's just a still life sketched on quite an ordinary day.

What brief illumination lights the darkened form.
Gifts the transient moment with the energy it needs
To make the journey from the mind to page.
From what is heard, observed and acted on life's stage.

The script of these brief years
Plays out our times of joy and sorrow.
Until there is no more tomorrow
On which to write our acts of peace and strife.

And in the end all that is left
Is just still life.

Going to the Doctors

She lifts her grandson from his seat,
Holds his perfect body to her chest.
Shifts him to her hip to better grip
His infant wriggle. Smiles at him with love
So deep and true. Absorbs the baby glory
Of his eyes, so clear and blue.

Side stepping, leaning in, she hauls her mother
From the seat which swallowed her,
Delivering her, one handed, out into the world
And somehow manages to lock the car,
Whilst, pivotal, between these two dependent beings
She wonders if her destination is a step too far.

And suddenly it strikes her, sounding deep
A clear, true existential thought
That on the road of time she stands,
In perfect juxtaposition to the 'shoulds' and 'oughts'
Of life; a timeless linking chain that's forged
By mother, infant, wife.

Brown Beauty

My brown eyed beauty treads the morning dew,
Bejewelled in diamond brilliance by the rising sun.
Rips at the sweet wet grass with tombstone teeth
And softly snorts her welcome to the day begun.

I throw my arms around her strong firm neck.
And she, so patient, interrupts her feast,
Lets me run my fingers up her dusty crest
To touch the strength and comfort of this lovely beast.

Her satin softness strokes my stroking hand
And we communicate with silent ease.
But I am sorrowfully aware
That there will be no further days like these.

For she must go to fields of well earned rest.
And I must grow to adulthood alone.
But I'll remember her, the sweetest and the best
Of childhood's comrades, my brown beauty. Bess.

Are there Horses in Heaven?

Are there horses in heaven? I hope so.
In fact, I insist there will be.
For I want to gallop on beaches
Which means that there has to be sea.
And if there is sea, there'll be sailing
In dinghies, so flighty and free
And the person who sails through the air or goes 'crash'
Just for once Lord, don't let it be me.

And if there are horses and beaches and seas
Please let there be dogs who will play
All together, with never a snarl or a growl
And please may there never be sand in my towel
In that glorious, wonderful place that will be
Where I shrug off this tatty old body and see
That the Lord who made horses is waiting for me.

Fred and Mary Married Sixty Years

When Fred and Mary come to mind
We feel the gentle tug of friendship's bonds,
A warm remembrance of a summer Sunday past
When food was offered, seasoned by such kind acceptance,
We were home at last.

For in their marriage there's a place
For that dear Presence who has blessed
Their combined gifts and talents,
Which Fred and Mary gently lace with love,
Allowing the free flowing of so many streams
Of Spirit filled abundance from above.

And now we celebrate with you
A marriage which in every sense so very few
Are to attain. In length and depth,
Up hills of trial and down the depths of fears,
They've kissed each other's hurts
And dried each other's tears.

And sixty years have passed
And in that time so many have rejoiced
When Fred and Mary have displayed a marriage
Oh, so full of faithfulness and truth
That they themselves are, of God's love,
The proof.

Thinking About Chewy, Marie Brewster's Cat

We miss them when they go.
Their non-judgemental friendship
Light our days and so we weep when,
With the passing time, they die.

Where do they go, these comrades of our years?
Is there some heavenly place where cats can purr
And lanky lurchers sleep on sofas, never moving
Unless they choose to do so. Only to run and run
Chasing celestial rabbits in joyful, friendly fun.

I do not know. In honesty I cannot say
Where goes the much loved friend
Who leaves today.
But God is kind and so I trust I'll see
That when I'm there in Heaven with Him
My faithful friend will be there too, with me.

Falling Out

It took me by surprise.
Dealt me a blow which I was unprepared for.
Left me sobbing in my wine
And with a heart pruned cruelly from the vine
No matter how I try or where I look
I can't avoid the fallout
From the road I took.

When was it then that clarity occurred?
Opened my eyes, my heart, my mind
That I could find the woman I must be
If I'm to walk into the Lord's pure light.
Accepting no more shadows
And with my Father's help in trembling honesty say
The truth at last, that I am gay.

Limpets

Limpet-like they cling to one another.
Each, having lost the rock, has found the other.
Sister to sister, brother to brother they cleave,
And cannot, for the life of them, each other leave.
Swept by raging tides they dance and sing
Whispering words which to the other bring
Comfort, safety, shelter in the storm
And lighten for a while the deepening darkness
Into which, by Fate's grim, careless hand
Each was born.

Who has the right to denigrate their peace.
To analyse and criticise their love
They've found a place of safety in their storm
Who knows it didn't come from God above?
Who has the right to say that they are wrong
That they should stay out in the cruel cold
And never find the home where they belong
And somehow count their blessings till they're old.

I find it sits more peacefully in my heart
If I consider what my Lord might do
When faced with this dilemma. Would He start
With rigid readings, withheld friendship too?
I think not. I cannot hold in mind
An image of a God aloof and far.
And Jesus knows that love between the two
Is not in what they do, but who they are.

Stolen Woman

I stole a woman. No, not all at once
But piece by piece and starting with her eyes
I knew she'd turn to me and, captured by my look
Would follow, eye to eye, with glad surprise.
Having seized her eyes I moved on to her hands
And saw, in their slim beauty, so much pleasure,
That slowly, at my leisure, I gently stroked her fingers
With my mind.
In the smooth satin of her skin, I found communion,
Wordless joy, that trembling with love
Having no mindfulness of sin
I opened wide my hard yet brittle heart and asked her in
To the very centre where not one soul before
Had touched, or stirred to life the lovefullness
Behind the door.

We Went to War

A Song

Listen! Do you hear it
There is music on the wind.
It's the sound of many voices
Raised in song, raised in song.
The young, the old, the brave, the bold
Who yearn to come along, come along.

Chorus

Join up! Join up! The voices cry.
Your country needs you, do or die.
We'll beat the enemy, by and by,
So come, come, come along.

And so we came, to play the game
With uniform and gun.
We did not know, of those who go
So few back home would come.
Back home, back home,
So few back home would come.

Chorus

Join up! Join up! We heard the cry
Your country needs you. Do or die
We'll beat the enemy, by and by
So come, come, come along

We started out so cheerfully.
We hushed our weeping wives.
We only thought quite fleetingly
That we ourselves might die.
We did not think. We did not think
That we ourselves might die.

But then we reached the battle ground
The truth stuck home as there we found
Our ears and eyes were plundered by
The horror all around.
Our ears and eyes were plundered by
The horror all around.

Chorus

Fight on! Fight on! Must be the cry.
Your country needs you. Do or die.
We'll beat the enemy by and by
Fight on. Fight on. Or die

The canons' roar, the sniper's shot,
The mustard gas. We had the lot.
And those of us who never pray
Called out to God on that bleak day
Called out to God, called out to God
On that bleak, dying day.

And we see all around us
Those we've fought beside this day
Are lying, dead and dying in the mud
They are lying dead and dying
And our very souls are crying
For our brothers who are dying in the mud.

So listen to our voices
That now whisper on the wind.
Remember us. Remember us we say.
And the question lingering on
Was it worth the price we paid
Is the tremble in the echo
Is the tremble in the echo
Is the tremble in the echo
As our voices fade away.

Soldier

He said 'good-bye' to Mother,
Waved a farewell to his wife.
Not knowing what the future held,
He pledged to risk his life
Defending King and Country
In some far off, foreign place.
For the honour of his nation
He would fight the other race.

But on the field of battle
In a flash of searing pain,
He saw his ageing mother
And kissed his wife again.
Shed his blood to feed the seeds of glory,
Shaken on that day,
Where later poppies leap to life,
Lift up their heads and say,
Remember each and every man
Who's lost his life since war began.
Those deaths of husbands, fathers, sons,
By snipers, bayonets and guns.

And if it is forgotten how
The whole thing came to be,
There is a man, at rest in France,
Remembered now, by me.
And oh, so many others
When they search their family tree,
And see the scarlet poppies
Where their loved ones used to be.

My Mum

She left me far too early, my mum,
Following my dad into the dark unknown
Where, someone told me, Heaven is.
I only knew that from then on
I was alone.

She packed for me, my mum,
A suitcase stuffed with ways to cope,
Some underwear of feelings, crushed and worn
But not much future,
Not much hope.

And she forgot, my mum,
To pack some vital things I should have known
Or maybe wasn't granted time enough
To stop me making big mistakes
Before I'd grown.

She didn't pack enough resolve, my mum,
To keep me from the hands of wicked men
Or confidence to know I could achieve,
Well, perhaps a little more had I but started
Way back then.

But what she did was pack with love, my mum,
Which strengthened me and brought me to this place
Where I can find some meaning and some peace
Glimpsing the resurrection of my mother's smile
In my own child's face.

The Lost Word

I am trying to remember a word!
A word which you will have heard me say
Again and again throughout the day.
But now it's just up and flown away!
What is that pesky word?

It's really quite common and not at all rare.
But now I can't find it, which seems most unfair.
I've happily used it most days until now,
Without any problem. How could I forget it?
I ask again! How?

But wait a minute, here it is.
The letter combination which caused such irritation
Because I could not find it in my mind.
But oh! No! Curses! Oh bother! What a pain!
That pesky word has flown!
It's gone again!

Characters and events in the Life of Jesus

These subjective glimpses into the journey Jesus made from his birth to his death are the result of my personal reflections. The events happened. Or not of course, depending on one's own conviction.

I have placed characters in situations where they may well have existed and granted them a voice which, Biblically speaking, they have been denied.

Joseph

What is this you are saying?
What words are these I've heard?
A child has been conceived by she
With whom I meant my life to be?
Now all my hopes and dreams are gone
As in the slamming of a door.
Because if what you say is true,
My Mary is a whore!

You say that God has done this!
I fear you are quite mad
Or simply making stories up
To hide the fact you're bad.
I need to spend some time alone
To think how it can be
That Mary, who I love so much,
Could do this thing to me.

And yet, I cannot bear to think,
Of you, my Mary, dead.
Stoned by righteous men of law
Because of what you've said.
And now, and now, the strangest dream.
An angel's come to me
And said I should not be afraid.
What is God's will, will be.

Oh Mary, this is, oh, so hard
But I am bound to you
By more than mortal bonds of love
And Yahweh's will, I'll do.
I'll try to be a father
And I promise on my life
I'll take you and protect you
As my own beloved wife.

And this small child, when born to us
As my own child will be.
And though he is just lent to us
I pray I'll live to see
The future, when He'll raise us up
Where God has said we'll be.
And so, my Mary, here and now
My words shall be my solemn vow.

The Midwife

How strange the light, I thought, as cold and tired
I hurried through the night.
Pushing past the gathering crowds of strangers
Census summoned, crowding into rooms so overbooked
That landlords, faces flushed with avarice
Looked quite unfamiliar
As though from some far gentile place,
Not Bethlehem, not my God fearing race.

It all seemed strange. And when I heard
The gut wrenched groan a woman makes
When it is time a new life to bring forth,
Then I was glad for this is what I know. My task. My skill.
And even though it led me to a stable door
I went inside and knelt beside the labouring child
Who lay there on the floor.

She seemed so young and looked at me with frightened eyes.
Her husband who could not quite disguise his fear,
Seemed glad to see a midwife near.
And so I stayed. And how I prayed that God would bless this child
And bring him safely forth.
Time went by and when at last a man child breathed our air
Oh do not scoff when I in truth declare
That I am certain there were angels there.

Herod

There is a clawing hand
Which grips my guts
With talons. Long and sharp,
That twist and twist until I want to scream
And every minute of the night and day
I hear, inside my head, my demons say
I am the King. No other shall there be.
And I will slaughter every newborn child
Who challenges me.

Call the soldiers. Tell them go
To this so insignificant hole
From where, according to those cursed seers,
A King of Kings will rise.
Oh, NO! For I will render him destroyed
Before he can.
And not one baby boy from Bethlehem
Will grow to be a man.

And will the screams of women touch my heart?
Or frantic fathers clinging to their sons
My conscience prick? Deny the thought!
So go now, and be quick to sweep away
The doomed imposter who would take my throne.
And not one inch will I surrender of this kingdom that I own.

Where is the boy?

We didn't know he'd gone.
Where is the boy?
Sometimes he's wild, like every child
But he would never mean to worry us.
To have us in this flurry,
Searching every place he might have been
Oh, has that son of ours been seen?

Where is the boy?
And now of all times, when so many thousand feet
Lift the dust of ages in the streets of old Jerusalem
And you and I, Mary, we feel again
Those fear filled memories from our past
When our small boy was in such peril
In dreams, by angels we were told
And saw the Lord's amazing plan unfold
With our son at its centre.
And now he's lost.
Where is the boy?

But here! But here at last he is!
Relief and anger mixed in equal parts.
Until his words our fear torn hearts now still.
'Where would you find me but within
The presence of my Father's will.'

The Watcher

Were we excited? Yes, of course we were.
We'd heard the prophet's promise all our lives
That our Messiah would come and lead us home.
Restore our lost position as the chosen race
And fill us once again with Yarweh's grace.
We knew He'd fight for us and that no force
Of empire, human or demonic, would succeed
In overcoming Him, the chosen One,
Promised to our forefathers from time begun.

But did this man called Jesus fight the fight?
Did he call up legions, break the foe
And onward into victory unchallenged go?
No he did not. For all his so called power.
Just fairy tales. God failed him in his dying hour.

So were we conned? I think perhaps we were.
And yet there was that certain something in the man
That made so many of us follow him.
Perhaps that's why I'm crying here today.
And why I feel compelled to stand and pray.
I've raised my eyes now to his dying face.
He's met my gaze with eyes so full of pain
That I can barely take in breath again.
For in that look I see no dread of death
But sorrow and compassion for this watching soul
And know that my redemption is his goal.

The Garden

We went to the garden that night
After the meal. We had been before
But this was different.
Well, we all knew that, had he not said
Such strange and awe filled words to us
That even my love flooded heart
Was drowned in dread.

I knew he was in pain.
I thought I knew him well
But when he bade us sit and wait,
That he would have some space
To think and pray,
I did not realise the agony of mind
That he would face before the day.

And so I slept. How could I
When this man I loved so much
Needed to know that those for whom
He gave his life, were by his side.
Awake. Alert. To hold within their hearts
His pain. His hurt.

And when his breaking voice rebuked us
Then I knew that all the triumph
That I thought would soon be ours,
Could not be gained without these anguished hours.
And even knowing this to my great shame,
When danger came, I did not stay.
But ran away.

The Man I Am

The Man I Am feels loneliness and pain.
And yearns sometimes a warm and human love.
But I am not the subject of such care
Because I do not come from here.
But up above.

The Man I Am feels hurt by human hands,
And deep rejection stabs my human heart.
And sometimes many hours of weary work
Drag down my steps and seek to bind
The divine part.

The Man I Am feels loss, both mine and yours
As He who sent me here can never do
But clothed in flesh my purpose here is this
To bring you to the Father
Him to you.

And so it is. But could I human be
If I did not sometimes look up and say
My Father, I will do your will but still might ask
That from my path should pass
This tortured day

Pilate

I've scrubbed and rubbed and all but taken
Off the skin which clothes my hands.
I've tried but still, with fingers bleeding
I just cannot understand
How it came to be that man
Went to his death at my command.

I tell myself there were no choices.
Tell myself no fault was mine.
Ignored my wife who dreamt of voices
Telling her he was divine.
But the people chose Barabbas
And I took the safer way.
But find no matter how I try
I cannot scrub the stain away.

And when I turn to my gods
To release me from this sin,
I feel no loving presence
As the love I sensed in him.
And when I have no answer
For the wrong that I have done,
Where will my household gods be then
When faced with Yahweh's Son?

Good Friday

Crush, bruise, curse, rage,
Degradation centre stage.

Friends run. Mother cry.
Sacrificed son die.

Side pierced. Blood shed.
Satan laughs. God dead.

Sky dark. Heart break.
Courage now. Just wait.

Mary at the Cross

My son. My son. Beloved one.
How could it come to this
When as a babe upon my breast
You lay so helpless in my arms
While all around, in boundless joy,
All Heaven rejoiced, my sweetest boy.

Though I was warned of pain to come
And knew you were not just my son
But of the Lord's ordaining, I forbade
All frightening visions of the years to come
And tried to claim you as my very own,
My lovely darling boy.
The Holy One, I'm forced to see,
Was by God's grace just lent to me.

And now, and now, what agony is this
To watch you tortured and to see you die.
Is this God's plan? However can that be
To sacrifice the child He placed in me?
What do I know? Just that I love you so
And claim the promise that the Lord gave me.
The babe I bore would the Messiah be.

John

I met a man who waited
Knowing there would be a word
That would drop into the silence
Deep inside.
That word, which he would recognise
As spoken just for him,
Would resonate far down
Where all his darkest sorrows hide.

He knew that he was trusted
With the mother of his Lord
To take her to his home and hold her grief.
With loving arms and broken heart
He'd do the best he could.
And with certainty much clearer
Than any he had known
He knew the Lord would claim him as His own.

Beloved, yes, Beloved was the word he heard that day
Through the pain and devastation in his heart.
And despite his human frailties, his weaknesses, his fears
He knew he'd have the strength to do his part.
For in that name, 'Beloved' was the essence of the role
He would play to the Glory of the Lord
And that same name, 'Beloved' is the promise to us all
That we too are the loved ones of the Lord.

Two Mothers

Oh Mary, as the time went by
Did you dread to see your son
The focus of the Pharisaic eye?
And did you know that he was
Bound to die?
I think you did.

And Mary, did that dreadful knowledge
On your every moment sit,
Eroding all your joy and laughter
Bit by bit?
And did you plead with him
Abandon it!
Perhaps you did.

But Mary, did you realise that
Just like you I had a son
With fearful visions too.
And watched him grow obsession
In his heart.
A man apart

And Mary, while your son
Walked his calling unto death,
My son's heart was ravaged by regret
That this was not the warrior of his dreams.
And so he lent his broken heart
To evil schemes.

These two young men
Both chose their day of death.
Mine a traitorous coward, yours a king.
And so I ask you Mary,
My son? Having played his part
In God's redemption scheme,
Will your redeemer son
My son redeem?

Didymus the Doubter

Didymus the doubter, well that is what they've said
When sometimes I have just not been convinced
That everything will turn out right,
That he is who they say,
For I am quite, quite certain
That he died on that dark day.

I saw his tortured body
As they took it from the cross.
And heard his mother sobbing in her agony of loss.
I watched his wounds no longer bleed,
His faltering heart grow still,
I knew that he could not come back
To life. And never will.

But then I came to be with them,
And in the upper room
They told me that he had been seen
And some of them had even been
With him! What! This cannot be,
Nor I believe, until I see with my own eyes
His living, breathing body.
Until then I fear that it is lies.

But now, what is this subtle bending of the air?
This sweet warm breath? This presence which I swear
Is Him. Is Him and I can see those wounds,
Those scars which He lays bare for me.
I cannot stand and I can hardly bear to see
His loving, holy eyes look down on me.

And so I worship Him with no regret,
No doubts, no ifs, no buts, no thoughts of any kind
And in this cleansing act of flesh and spirit find
My every question answered. No fears can stand
The touch upon my head of God's own hand.

Talking to God: More Question than Answers.

I have talked to God all my life. It has not been an easy relationship at times and I cannot imagine why He hasn't got fed up with me by now.

I've asked so many questions, argued so many angles and travelled to the boundaries of faith. And back again.

And yet He has been so gracious to me, not always answering my questions but assuring me that it is perfectly alright to ask them.

And so here are some final offerings; poems full of grief and anxiety, assurance and hope. Even some laughs. Well maybe. As in everything else, you can make up your own mind about that.

God Blog

It was on the Monday morning
That I got fed up with God
And thought I'd write and tell Him so
On my new laptop blog.

I tapped out my frustration,
How I think He doesn't care.
And that when it comes to trouble
I get far more than my share.

By Tuesday I'd developed
A very angry theme.
And blogged that if He bothered me
Again, I'd really scream.

By Wednesday I was screaming.
My blog throbbed with my ire.
I felt that my relationship with God
Was really dire.
Come Thursday I'd calmed down a bit
And shed a few sad tears.
And wrote that I was sorry
To give way to stupid fears.

My laptop broke on Friday.
P'raps God had had enough
Of my ranting and my raging
And my silly ego stuff.

'Get up from that computer'
I heard a quiet voice say.
'Sit down here beside me,
You needn't even pray.'

'Now quieten down your fearful soul.
And still your anxious mind.
No need to blog, or even tweet.
I really do not mind.

I don't require technology,
Theology, psychology
Or any other 'ology'
Which clutters up your mind.'

Come Saturday and Sunday
Once more I'm back on track.
I'm talking to our Father
And he is talking back.

If I just wait

If I just wait, will you come,
Rippling the surface of my silence with your breath?
Will you step into the chasm of my mind
And place your powerful presence
Between me and death?

If I can pray, will you hear?
Stretch your holy ear towards my tiny whimper.
And answer me, that silent whisper I perceive
When calmer frames of mind
Let me receive.

But just right now I cannot wait, or pray.
I cannot still my sobbing, hurting heart
Or see a different ending to my day
Than one which never really
Gives you every part.

And if I rage, will you then turn away,
Folding in your everlasting arms against this child.
Or will you, holding me in ancient, patient Love
Remind me that my destiny is not below.
But far above

So I will wait and pray and listen in the dark.
An act of will for now, if not the truth,
And try to trust that you have come, have heard, have held,
And all life's love is in itself, the proof.

Surrender

I've heard you, Lord, I've heard you,
Your quiet, persistent voice
Has reached my ears throughout the years
And always with a choice.
To shrug you off and walk away
Or stay before your gaze and pray.

You never have insisted.
Sometimes I wished you would.
So often did I turn and run,
Just because I could.
Freedom is a precious thing but often I've abused
Its glorious potential by the methods I have used
To keep my distance, go my way
And stubbornly refuse to pray.

But then one day, despite my fears,
Self centred misery and tears
For someone else's sake I prayed.
In naked pain, stripped of my pride
To myself at last I died.
And then your voice became a song,
A hymn of praise and all I long
To do or be is give at last
In full surrender all that's me.

The Day of Prayer

We sit in silence, waiting for your voice,
The whisper in our ear; the written word,
And when we hear you how our hearts rejoice
For we are sure our prayers to you are heard.

But what of those Lord God who wait in vain?
Who feel their pleas lie dying at your feet.
They fear that you know nothing of their pain.
And are convinced their needs you will not meet.

Hold out your hand to them, I hear you say.
For in your touch they will somehow feel mine.
And walk beside them on their hard trod way.
But do not try their answers to define.

For stepping stones along the way you are.
And you may never get to see their journey's end.
But you have held the door of love ajar
And when the time is right their hurts I'll mend.

Then they will come to me, their lives renewed.
No stage upon their journey missed or lost.
Finally the finished record will be viewed
And seen, though long and hard, well worth the cost.

Grief

Oh God

What is this life that we must feel such pain
When those we love cast off their chains and fly
Beyond our understanding, out of reach.
Is it the dark which claims us when we die?

What is this loss that we are forced to take
Another breath and walk on in our lives alone.
And yet hold out our hands to you in faith
And trust that, in due time, you'll lead us home.

There are no easy answers. But this we know.
Our lives are challenging journeys from the start
With joys and sorrows, happiness and pain
Enough to test the stoutest human heart.

A Question of Christmas

How bleak this winter's day.
How burdened with our fears.
Bleached pale and stark with grim dark news
And iced with frozen tears.
Where can we go for the answer
To all our human need?
To find some kindness and mercy
To balance our human greed.

Can we bear to open a stable door
And kneel with awe on the stable floor?
Reach out and take with our sin stained hands
The tiny hand of God?
Can we lift the Child from the manger?
Give Him space to grow in our hearts?
Nurture ourselves in His nature
And grow to be children of God?

Can we see through the glitter and glamour
To the wonderful truth that's within?
And believe that the Child in the manger
Is the God who is clothed in our skin?
Look at the gifts that He brings us.
Redemption, forgiveness and love,
And see in the eyes of this baby
The face of the Father above.

Can You Hear the Bells?

Can you hear the bells?
The chattering children's voices carolling joy?
A guiding star. The leap to life fulfilled
And swaddled in a manger, God's own baby boy.

Can you hear the bells?
The ting a ling of cashiers calling 'next!'
'Number eight please'. Frantic shoppers
Bring your goods this way
There's hardly any time till Christmas Day.

Can you hear the bells?
An urgent message from a sorrowful God,
My gift to you at Christmas was my Boy
You careless children broke him as you would a toy.
You thought you had grown out of him. That he was just for when
You were little infants. So not for now. Just then.
But oh my precious loved ones, how is it you don't see
That when I gave my son to you
My gift to you was me.

Can you hear the bells?
Calling you to turn your heart again
To ancient truths of peace, acceptance, love
Receive the gift this time with open mind
Unwrap it. Take down deep inside your soul
The glorious love and joy which you will find.

When will you come back, Lord?

(a prayer)

Two thousand years now since you came.
Representing yourself in human form.
A sacrificial ransom for the sin of man
That had held us in death's grip
Since life began.

But when will you come back Lord?
You left us with a vision
Of how things might have been
If only we had never sinned.
Had known the Kingdom from the start.
But something planted deep in us
An evil heart.

Most of us just stand and watch
As all across the world
Our fundamental greed for power,
The filthy ends of wicked means
Are never checked and rampage on.
Or so it seems.

So when will you come back Lord?
And sweep away the agony.
The dreadful fear that little human beings feel
Caught up like sprats in tangled nets.
Quite innocent. Oh the longer that you leave it Lord,
The worse it gets.

And those of us who know you
We struggle every day
With thoughts like these, of when and how
You might come back
And put an end to all this pain.
Oh Father God, Lord Jesus,
Come again.

A Voice in the Wilderness

They take my honest words, commence to shred them.
Chew them up and spit them out again.
Reconstituted, weakened by intention
To render them less powerful, more absurd.

Not facing up to truth when it disturbs them
But squeezing it to fit a narrow grave.
The burial of honest exploration
That tells me to be silent and behave.

For my belief won't fit their stunted vision
That states the Lord grants grace to only those
Who follow, word for word, man's reinvented
Laws of Love no early brethren heard.

Can they not feel the Spirit's gentle leading
Towards a fresh conception of the truth
That Christ became a man like us to save us,
Because we needed living, dying proof.
That nothing in creation can evict us
From standing in the context of His love
And claiming, as our own, the grace He gives us
To take our place in heavenly realms above.

Where is my Samaritan?

A song.

I am lying in the street in the city of my mind,
In the concrete urban jungle where the passers-by are blind
To my pain and desperation and the agony I'm in.
No Samaritan is passing by, no Jean or Jeff or Jim.

So I'm stuck here in the muck here. I'm really in the bin.
There's no dearth of spiritual gurus. All they talk about is 'sin'.
There's no loving in their ministry, no compassion in their eyes.
Just 'have a zap of this, sister!' and I think it's all lies.

The local boy evangelist says he knows what to do.
But all his frantic praying only puts me in a stew.
And when the powerful lady vicar blames my attitude of mind,
I'd like to take my bible and bash her big behind.

So, where is my Samaritan? What's happened to him Lord?
Does he have to make a judgement before I can be cured?
You said you don't break bending reeds. You tend the weak
and frail.
If there isn't any loving then the ministry will fail.

*If you fancy this to music dig out that dusty old guitar, play around with
D, G and A chords and think, 'YAHOO!'*

The Shepherd

Mantled by years, so many now have passed,
The shepherd stands, hunched back, his staff in hand.
And tends his master's flock with waning strength
But all the power of faith at his command.

For day by day through years both good and bad
The Spirit of the Living Lord has come
And stretched the pastures of this man of God
To gather in those seeking for the Son.

As high on craggy hills he's found lost sheep
And carried them to safety down below.
Or lifted to their feet those mired by pain
And placed them on a better path to know.

And all this time so many lives he's touched.
Has been the hands of Christ, has lived the Word.
Has laboured through his life with no reward
Save that of living as a shepherd of the Lord.

Africa... For Three Voices

Voice One
From the red murram soil of the east lands
To the vast sandy reach of the north.
Or deep underground in the southern veldt,
We cannot imagine your worth.
For you cradle the bones of our babies
And weep as our hopes and dreams wane.
And the Father of all our potential
Looks on in despair at our pain.
For we, where creation was cradled,
Stand now in the graveyard of loss
And the monsters of war and starvation
Join the beasts of disease as they toss
All the bones of intention between them
Till it seems that pure evil is boss.

Voice Two
But we who have wealth and good fortune,
Who wake with the hope every day
Of a reasonable lifetime before us,
Of good health and some fun, work with pay.
What can we do we might wonder
For our brothers and sisters like you?
When you make us feel queasy and guilty

And our own worries here are not few.
Oh we pray for you. Sometimes quite often.
And we give what we feel that we can.
But our purses get smaller and smaller
And don't quite live up to our plan.

Voice Three
But when our plans fail it is our fault.
God needs us to do all we can.
Be His hands, His feet, His compassion
In supporting the cradle of man.
When we give all we can to another
And he gives his all to a third,
Then our prayers have the voice of conviction
And the strength of our passion is heard.
For to carry the burden of Africa
We must be prepared for the pain
Of fighting the war on the Lord's side
Again and again and again.

If I Became an Ant Today

If I became an ant today
Would I perceive their pain?
And maybe have an ant's eye view
Of ant life; loss and gain?
Would I then have a broader view
And not a narrow eye,
Should I give up my human rights,
To live as ant, and die.

Is this what you have done for us
From your eternal throne?
Narrowed your omnipotence,
Left your heavenly home.
To spend a short, hard, human life,
To see things through our eyes.
To hear with human ears our words,
Our laughter and our cries.

Did you then know our deepest self?
The struggle raged inside.
That fights to keep the surface clean
And all the badness hide.
And do you have compassion Lord
Perhaps more than before
As I might if I could become
An ant down on the floor.

Mind Monkeys

I cannot control my thoughts Lord
And no matter what I do
They laugh and chatter at me
Like monkeys in a zoo.
They swing through the trees, screaming at me
In the forest that grows in my mind.
And without the slightest trouble
Leave all good intentions behind.

When I pass Mrs X in the street Lord
And no smile on her face do I see,
I try to think she's unhappy
And isn't just scowling at me.
But quick as a flash in my head comes
The thought that I think that she's thought,
That I am not worthy of notice
As I do not behave as I ought!

I think that these monkeys can speak Lord
To each other across the divide
And communicate, one to another,
Their intention to make us unkind.
But I feed them with judgemental thinking
And tuck them up snug in their bed
With my slowness to be more repentant
For the cruel things I've thought, but not said.

So Lord, when I hear the mad chatter
Of monkeys let loose in my mind,
Please help me to see that it matters
That it's not just the surface that's kind.
I must seriously cut down their rations
Put them on a diet that is strict
But I know that however I struggle
There's no way that I'll get this thing licked.

So I'll just have to do what I can Lord
And refuse to play games with the things
And try not to offer them titbits
Or build them new playpens and swings
And if, despite my endeavours
They are still not consigned to the bin
There is always the final solution
Which the nice local vet can bring in!

Words

Words are waiting in the wings
For their moment on the stage.
Words of gentleness and rage.

Words released in flocks and flying,
News of birth, of life, of dying,
A single sob of lost love. Crying.

Words then carry to the hearing
All that human hearts are fearing.
Also some intent on cheering.

Through the babble, spoken, written
Somewhere will God's truth be heard.
He will have the final Word.